AFFIRMATIONS FOR VALUES AND CHARACTER DEVELOPMENT

Tanisha Graham

Published by Jabneh Production Limited
Sterling, Grange Hill P.O.
Westmoreland, Jamaica, W.I.
ISBN 978-976-95952-3-1
For worldwide distribution

Printed in the United States of America
First Printing, 2018

DEDICATION

To the God of heaven who affirmed me, aided in the development of my values and continues to form my character.

FOREWORD

The context of today's world makes this strategic and creatively compiled list of affirmations a critical tool in the hands of educators, parents, guardians and other stakeholders, who are entrusted with the task of developing children and young people who are constantly bombarded by negative messages in a world that is increasing in darkness and what seems like an endless flow of a variety of distortions. This trend is causing many of our children and young people to live lives filled with low self-esteem and unawareness of individual worth, while drifting through life without any real sense of purpose and destiny.

These negative messages, which are constantly targeting the young generation via ads, movies, music, social media and other forms of communication, promote distorted concepts of beauty, success and contrary values and principles which will only serve to undermine the accurate development of character, emotions, sexuality and spirituality.

Miss Tanisha Graham seeks to lead her readers through a powerful process of self-discovery, and the development, consolidation and benefits of a well-built, balanced and solid character. At the epicenter of this process is faith in the Creator of us humans, who has the full and correct knowledge of what a properly functioning human should look like.

This is excellent material for all of our education institutions.

For those who are reading and engaging this process, this book can change your life — forever. Please allow me to welcome you to 'the new you'.

— **Pastor Wesley C. Boynes**
Chairman,
Northgate Youth and Family Development Foundation
Immediate Past-President,
Jamaica Independent Schools Association

Contents

Dedication iii

Foreword v

Introduction 1

Appreciation 3

Belief 4

Commitment 6

Diligence 8

Excellence 9

Forgiveness 10

Governance of Self 13

Humility 15

Integrity and Justice 17

Kindness 19

Love 20

Mindfulness 21

Nobility 23

Obedience 24

Positivity 25

Quietude 27

Respect 28

Strength 29

Truthfulness and Trustworthiness 30

Understanding 32

Vigilance 34

Willingness 35
eXemplary Lifestyle 36
Yielded 38
Zeal 40
About the Author 41

INTRODUCTION

These affirmations are for the childlike and mature in heart. It is for the childlike, as the enquiring nature characteristic of a childlike spirit is necessary for character formation and development.

The affirmations are also for the mature or open-hearted because it takes a mature, open-hearted approach to reflect on one's life, admit that adjustment is necessary and embrace new ways of affirming personal values and character change.

Appreciation

I am appreciative.

This means:

I am thankful for the relationships God has given me.
I genuinely appreciate the things others do to contribute to my life and growth.
I do not take the people God has placed in my life for granted.
I am glad that I am alive.
I am grateful for the opportunities God has given to me.
I will use my thoughts, ideas, words, responses, actions, work and life to show how appreciative I am.
My life will say out loud that I am truly grateful.
It will say thank you.

Belief

I believe.

This means:

My faith is alive.

It is constant.

It will cause me to triumph.

My confidence is completely invested in God.

Therefore,

My spirit will not succumb to negativity.

My mind will not be overtaken by darkness and despondency.

My soul will not be penetrated by cynicism.

The unknown will not intimidate me.

Challenges will not make me anxious or cause me to doubt.

I will remain faithful.

I will not allow fear to cause me to digress from the path God has ordained for my life.

I do not know where this new path may lead but I rise up in my spirit and

I face the encounters of this new way.

I know that I will be one step closer to completing my God-given assignment.

I am confident that once God is my guide and partner, He will cause every circumstance and every obstacle to propel me in the direction He wants me to go.

I am an overcomer.

I will fulfil my purpose in the face of negative, doubtful and hateful people who have already determined that I will fail.

I will try even when others think I am already out.

I press on to achieve my dreams in spite of challenging circumstances.

I will succeed in adding beauty to the world despite a disappointing past, negative experiences, or other mitigating circumstances.

I will not give up on myself despite injury, hurt and tests. I will continue to shine in the place in which I have been ordained to stand.

My resolve and faith will not fail.

Commitment

I am committed.

This means:

I am resolute.

I will not turn back.

I am no longer wavering.

I have made up my mind.

It's a done deal.

I must follow through and stick this out to the end.

I honour my promises even if it costs me to do so.

Hence, I must know what is worthy of giving my word and myself for and to.

I carefully consider before I commit to the process.

I do not give my words or my heart freely or precipitously.

I give consideration before I speak.

If I give my word, part of me has been given to fully implement what I said I would do.

If I give my word, my heart, my life and my time are already given.

For these reasons, I commit only to purposeful, meaningful things.

My life is of significant value; therefore, I honour that life by engaging in and committing to things that lead to my adding true value to the world in which I live.

DILIGENCE

I am diligent.

This means:

I take small steps so I can move towards fulfilling my goals.
I do not wait until the last moment to start or to complete tasks which have been assigned to me.
I make use of available opportunities to thoroughly prepare.
I am a hard worker who is busy doing purposeful and fruitful things.
I have an advantage as I pay careful attention to details that add value to the whole picture.
I keep practising, planning and thoroughly preparing for the future.

Excellence

I am an excellent person.

This means:

I am not just one who does an excellent job;
I excel in my attitude, speech, work, conduct, character and life.
The framework from which I operate is one of giving my best.
I give my best effort in spite of doubters, critics and sceptics.
I recognize personal mediocrity is not an option.
I do things with all my might.
I perform and operate at the highest ethical standards, whether someone is watching or not.
I do not need to compete with others; I just give my best.
I accomplish things with all the vibe and energy that reverberate within me.
I will therefore give my best effort to my relationships and the tasks that are set before me, no matter how insignificant they seem.

FORGIVENESS

I am forgiving.

This means:

I forgive myself.
I release myself from the mistakes I made.
I pardon myself from the stupid and unconscionable things I did in the past.
I apologize to myself for allowing others to take advantage of me.
I seek forgiveness from myself for my carelessness; for not seeing myself as valuable as I should have,
For not seeing my life as a sacred and valued trust committed to me and which must be guarded and superintended.
I forgive others.
I release others from the ridiculous and cruel things they said or did to me.
Since I have released all those who have hurt me,
I release the onlookers who others believe were supposed to come to my help and did not.
My heart is like my Father God's and it is big enough,

So I even release the flawed systems of earthly justice and authority figures that others say were supposed to redress situations and did not.
I give my hurting heart and unresolved situations to God, and like my Father God, I absolve them of their wrongs.
Let their wrongs fall upon their own heads if they choose to continue in it, but I release them from whatever they have done to me.
I will not be miserable, bitter and angry because of them.
I refuse to constantly remind myself and others about their past wrongs, especially when they have moved on.
I refuse to hold a grudge and contaminate my heart with bad blood.
I hate wickedness, but I refuse to infect my heart with vengeful thoughts and actions;
I will let God deal with that.
I will not cast my stone;
I will use that stone as the cornerstone or foundation for my new life.
I will act wisely in my future relationships.
I will not wait for an apology in order to forgive (if they are truly cruel, I will be waiting too long).
I do not need an explanation for what they did or did not do and why they did it before I forgive them.

My explanation is that they are human beings, not God.

I do not need the world's idea of closure; I already got closure when I forgave them,
And so I am moving on....

Governance of Self

I govern myself.

This means:

I control myself.
I take charge of my life.
I walk forward to embrace my destiny.
I set boundaries for myself.
I mind my own business.
I keep watch over things in my jurisdiction.
I govern my state.
I cast off indecency and reject lawlessness.
I listen to God's law.
I interpret and apply His standards for my life.
I execute and enforce His laws in my domain.
I incarcerate and put to death my wrong attitudes and toxic mental postures.
I re-train my mind and correct my behaviour.
I restrain myself from any attempt to blame, control or manipulate others.
I begin to change.
I rule over my spirit.
I put myself in my place.

I subdue my appetite, control my tongue and discipline my body.
I wisely rule over my emotions, desires and passions. They will not overrun my life.
I enslave all my faculties and demand they come into alignment with what is good and noble.
I subject my life to principle and purpose to embrace the order which comes with God's complete governance of my life.

HUMILITY

I humble myself.

This means:

I understand that there is a higher authority than myself and I submit to it.
I acknowledge that my strength comes from a higher place—a place beyond me. I will not forget that.
I know I need God.
I need Him to succeed, prosper and be humble.
I am desperately and forever dependent on Him.
I have been endowed with knowledge, talents, wealth, ingenuity, influence and power. I understand that these things can only be appropriately managed and purposefully wielded when I re-submit them to the Master who entrusted me with them in the first place.
I recognize the glory should be given to the Creator who gave me breath and in no way do I try to camouflage that.
It belongs to Him;
I am a steward and I humble myself.
I refuse to be condescending.

I refuse to exploit the weaknesses of others, even when I have the absolute advantage.
I will not interact with others from a prideful or lofty position.
I will relate with people who others deem to be in unfortunate circumstances or of lower status.
I will do this without being uncomfortable or making them uncomfortable.
I will always be more intent on adding value than in my receiving adulation.
I recognize that by myself, I can be deceived and so I cannot have myself, my emotions, nor my thoughts as a final authority. I must trust God to be that for me and to direct me.
I humble myself.

Integrity and Justice

I embody integrity and justice.

This means:

There is no duplicity.
I am one.
I am not disjointed.
I am whole.
I am good to the core.
I am bound not just by duty, but my conscience.
I can be trusted to do what is morally upright and to execute that which is superiorly good.
I am free from treachery and deception.
I am riveted with good things deep down inside me.
I am uncompromising in my values.
I am fair.
I am honourable.
I refuse to have my opinions and thoughts shaded by material gain.
I cannot be bribed.
I cannot be bought or swayed with anything except the unswerving timeless value of what is noble, good, superior, principled and honourable.

I stand firm in my resolve with integrity in my heart, mind and actions.
I will not live in a manner that deviates from the values I know to be true, wise and tested.
I will not be a coward. I will not allow people, relationships, family, friends or the world to influence me into compromising good and entering a dark realm.
Corruption will have no place in my life.
With God's help, I will remain pure, true and uncompromising.

Kindness

I am kind.

This means:

I am kind-hearted.
I use kind words.
I think kind thoughts.
I use my hands to do kind things.
My kindness will be seen in my refusal to say everything I think and feel.
I am considerate.
I speak only the words that uplift the mind and spirit of others.
I refuse to be mean and judgemental towards others, whether in thought or action.
I give others the benefit of the doubt. I refuse to be cynical or sarcastic in my comments.
I will not jeer or demean others.

I will be respectful.

Love

I am loving.

This means:

I have a loving heart.
I have a loving mind.
My posture is one of love.
I choose to love myself.
I choose to love others.
I am considerate of others.
I am kind.
I am sacrificial and unselfish in nature.
I demonstrate love to others with my words.
I demonstrate love to others with my actions.
I ensure the motivation for my actions is the enhancement of my fellow men.
I seek their highest good.
I remain committed to their wellbeing.
They are significant to me.

MINDFULNESS

I am mindful.

This means:

I am present and alert.
I am fully conscious, aware and engaged in life.
I am not emotionally, spiritually nor relationally sedated.
Even though things may be happening very swiftly, I choose to participate and to make a contribution to my world.
I am mindful of my character.
I am mindful of my strengths, my weaknesses and my need to mature.
I consciously evaluate what kind of person I am and who I want to become.
I consistently consider how I wish to live.
I am mindful of my surrounding context and the various needs.
I am attentive to my brothers and sisters.
I am aware of their physical and emotional circumstances.
I am conscious of the compassion I need to develop to aid them in their plight.

I will carefully consider, reflect on and evaluate the systems, people and places I wish to impact.
I am mindful of the choices I must make in order to become a person who adds value to this world.

Nobility

I am noble.

This means:

I am upright and decent.
I am a good person.
I take the high road.
My attitude and my conduct are above reproach.
I have pure thoughts about myself and others.
I do not hold on to contaminated or selfish motives.
My intentions are wholesome.
My heart remains pure.
I am appropriate in my conversations and in the way I conduct myself.
I pursue that which is right and fair.
Even in my thoughts, I uphold that which adds value to my fellow human beings.

Obedience

I am obedient.

This means:

When I hear the voice of God in my spirit, I obey.
When I hear His voice through my family, my teachers and friends, I follow His lead.
I surrender to what God is saying, knowing that His call is more potent than my own ideas of what I think I should be or do.
I resist all attempts to do my own thing.
I submit to God because I believe obedience to God's will is a call to higher ways and greater things; it is a call to develop my character.

Positivity

I am positive.

This means:

I believe the best about the future.
I remain positive even when surrounding situations look difficult.
I remain hopeful in the midst of my challenges.
I will not murmur nor complain.
I view things from my Creator's positive paradigm.
I think about the good things that are possible.
I refuse to become entrapped by negative attitudes, positions and philosophies.
I reject negative thoughts and vibes.
I stop negativity in its tracks. I will not be overrun by rotten emotional and mental garbage.
Negative people do not rule over me; they do not control my life.
I create a positive space with my positive words, actions and life.
My positive nature neutralizes toxic forces and arguments.

Despite how sordid things may seem, I keep my mind stayed on positive, noble, honorable things that generate peace, harmony and goodwill.

QUIETUDE

I embody quietude.

This means:

Tranquility is mine.
Stillness is mine.
I am centered.
I am at rest internally.
My heart and mind are at peace.
There is neither war nor turbulence inside of me.
I have a quiet spirit.
I do not have to war, manipulate, scheme and plot to accomplish things or get attention.
I have God's attention.
I trust Him to work out things for my good.
I will remain still.
In stillness, I find true confidence.
In stillness, holy thoughts are given to me.
In stillness, I transcend my life of burden.
In stillness, I remember my values.
In stillness, I see who I truly am.

Respect

I am respectful.

This means:

I respect myself.
I respect my body, soul and spirit.
I respect the breath and speaking of God coming to and through me.
I respect the energy, creativity and life the Creator has infused in me.
I respect that so much that
I do not surrender my soul, thoughts, gifting, destiny and principles for material things or to please other people.
I respect you.
I have high regard for your life and personhood—soul, mind, spirit and body.
I refuse to demean you.
I will be courteous, respectful and mannerly towards you.
I do not need to be rude to get my point across.
I will respect you.

Strength

I am strong.

This means:

I am empowered.
I am built for this.
I have a robust spirit.
I am armored on the inside.
I am reinforced with internal strength, which comes from above.
My spirit has been secured, my soul protected and my mind fortified.
I will not break.
Pressure does not break me.
Criticism does not devastate me.
Conflict does not overwhelm me.
Heartbreak does not kill me.
Crisis does not crush me.
Loss does not weaken me.
Adversity does not stop me.
I am resilient.
I have the capacity to break and change things with my resolve,
And my resolve is very strong.

Truthfulness and Trustworthiness

I embody truthfulness and trustworthiness.

This means:

I speak the truth;
I live out the truth.
I live authentically.
I refuse to falsify my world.
I do not shrink back from who God says I truly am.
I truly live out what I believe God says about me.
I cannot live in pretense.
I live truth, fully.
I understand that God has given me a trust of which I must prove myself worthy.
I appreciate the fact that He has put His confidence and faith in me.
I am sensitive to the fact that I have His heart in my hand and I cannot deal with Him deceptively.
I recognize that He could have refused to trust me, so I will not take His trust for granted or deliberately let Him down.

He has put His name and reputation on the line because He believes that I will treat His trust with care.
He has given me the benefit of the doubt.
He is relying on me.
Therefore, I will not shrink back from my responsibility.
His trust inspires me to honour Him by being trustworthy.

UNDERSTANDING

I am understanding.

This means:

My perspective of a situation is balanced with compassion, humility and the thought that I may not fully know what someone is facing.
I am not so caught up in my false world of reality that I cannot see what others are experiencing.
I recognize I am human and I could have been in their circumstance.
I may not fully understand them or the situation, but I will try to.
I am considerate, gentle, and accommodating, especially at such a difficult time in other people's lives.
Therefore:
I refuse to condemn and accuse.
I restrain myself from swiftly offering solutions, presenting opinions, imparting perspectives and making harsh judgements and conclusions.
Instead, I quickly offer my patience, my ears to listen and my heart to understand.

I patiently listen to what others have to say, not just with their lips but with their heart.

Vigilance

I am vigilant.

This means:

I keep close watch over the affairs of my life.
I observe and listen keenly to what is happening in my context and my world.
I guard the things for which I have responsibility.
I sharply pursue my relationships, my goals and the development of my character in a manner that allows me to know and see what is going on.
I will myself into doing what is required for me to become aware of what I am in charge of.
I am not slothful, passive, intoxicated nor mentally anaesthetized.
I am not consumed by things that cause me to become too engrossed or unconscious to things requiring my keen attention and which are of value to me.
I am alert.

WILLINGNESS

I am willing.

This means:

I do not need to be coerced nor induced.
I do not need to be pleaded with, encouraged, manipulated nor paid.
I do not have to be brow-beaten nor argued with.
I see the nature of it all and I am willing.
I am self-motivated.
I am doing this of my own accord.
I want to do this.
I am mentally prepared to do this.
I am eager to rise up.
I am enthusiastic about changing.
I am prepared to grow.
I am ready to share.
I willingly give myself to God.
I willingly expend myself to achieve His purpose and His goals.

eXEMPLARY LIFESTYLE

I lead an exemplary life.

This means:

I am a good example.
I appreciate that what I believe and who I really am is evident not just through my words but in my conduct.
My imagination, thoughts, words and actions represent the goodness that is left in the world.
My lifestyle is a brilliant illustration of what is honourable, decent, and pure.
My actions are positive reminders of the good things that are possible.
I do not live in a vacuum.
My behaviour does affect others.
I influence others directly and indirectly.
My thoughts, attitude, and mentality affect the emotions, behaviour and outlook of others.
My words and lifestyle influence and generate activity.
They evoke thoughts, create emotions, and produce intents and actions that were not present before.

My walking and working through hardship is evidence of God's power to preserve.
I therefore have a significant part to play in visibly representing and reminding others of the value of the grace of God on one's life.
I am an indication of God's power to affect an otherwise ordinary life.
Therefore, I must live in a manner which brings glory to my Creator.
My behavior must be worthy of emulation.
I must lead an exemplary life.

Yielded

I am yielded.

This means:

I yield to the will of my Maker.
There is neither fighting nor resistance.
I reject rebellion.
I say yes to God, not just with my words but with my heart and life.
I submit to His perfect will as in my heart I know He has a superior plan.
I affirm His sovereignty in my life.
I accept His covering.
I follow His leadership.
I am pliable in His hand.
I submit to Him crafting, molding and shaping my life.
I resist all attempts to go my own way and to follow my own will.
I relinquish my own understanding and idea of what is best for me.
I defer to God's preferences, thoughts, intents and musings.

I accept His reformation of my character.

I am inundated by His love.

I welcome an obedient heart.

I willingly surrender to His embrace.

I affirm His will for my life.

I yield.

ZEAL

I am zealous.

This means:

I am excited.
I am passionate.
I want to get it done.
I am motivated.
I want to be purposeful.
I want to be productive.
You do not need to light a fire under me;
It has already been lit from within.

THE END

About the Author

Tanisha Graham is passionate about affirming and practically implementing values and attitudes in her own life. Her book is an attempt to share with others her own reflections and affirmations so they, too, can ultimately realign their lives with their own personal values.

www.ingramcontent.com/pod-product-compliance
Ingram Content Group UK Ltd.
Pitfield, Milton Keynes, MK11 3LW, UK
UKHW040028200726
13854UKWH00001B/417